Handwriting
Activity Book

for ages 6-7

This CGP book is bursting with fun activities to build up children's skills and confidence.

It's ideal for extra practice to reinforce what they're learning in primary school. Enjoy!

Handwriting Hints

1) Sit up straight at your desk or at a table.

2) Get a grown-up to help you hold your pencil properly. Use your right or left hand — whichever you find easier.

3) Some pages have a big example of joined-up letters at the top. Use the red arrows to help you trace the join. Then you can practise the join with different letters on the lines underneath.

4) Use the lines to help you keep your letters neat. They will show you where your letters should sit, and where the top and bottom of each letter should be.

5) Work neatly. Try to keep your letters the same size.

Hints for Helpers

Here are a few things to bear in mind when using this book:

- Every school has its own handwriting style. Some schools may form letters and joins differently to how they're written here. Check with the school to see how they write and join each letter.

- As well as joined-up handwriting, this book covers break letters, which aren't joined to other letters. Some schools have different break letters (for example, g can be a break letter or it can be joined up). Check which break letters the school uses.

- Throughout the book, the red dots show where to start writing. As well as a red dot, the first example of each type of join has arrows to follow.

- It's best to work through the book in order — it gets harder as you go through, and later pages build on content covered earlier.

Contents

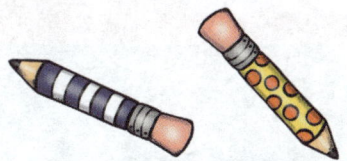 

Handwriting hobbies	2
Joining to small letters	4
Joining to e	6
Joining small and tall letters	8
Joining to round letters	10
Joining from the top	12
Puzzle: Distract the dragon	14
More joining from the top	16
More joining round letters	18
Break letters	20
Capital letters	22
A trip to the supermarket	24
Build your own robot	26
Space stories	28
Answers	30

Published by CGP

Editors: Rachel Craig-McFeely, Catherine Heygate, Katya Parkes, Rebecca Russell

With thanks to Alison Griffin and Jack Tooth for the proofreading.

With thanks to Jan Greenway for the copyright research.

ISBN: 978 1 78908 535 8

Printed by Elanders Ltd, Newcastle upon Tyne.
Cover and graphics used throughout the book
© www.edu-clips.com
Cover design concept by emc design ltd.

Text, design, layout and original illustrations
© Coordination Group Publications Ltd. (CGP) 2020
All rights reserved.

Photocopying this book is not permitted, even if you have a CLA licence.
Extra copies are available from CGP with next day delivery • 0800 1712 712 • www.cgpbooks.co.uk

Handwriting hobbies

How It Works

Before we get stuck into joined up writing, let's get warmed up with some words that will help you practise all the letters of the alphabet.

Use the lines to make sure your letters are the right size.

The red dots show you where to start each word.

Now Try These

1. Can you trace these words?

    reading

    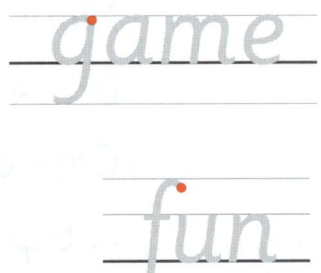 game

   books

   fun

2. Now see if you can trace and then copy each of the hobbies below.

    football  puzzles

    music

2

3. Trace and copy the sentences below. Start each word at the red dot.

Tim skates quickly.

She went for a jog.

Devi loves to exercise.

An Extra Challenge

Can you work out what each person's hobby is? Choose from the words in the box.

baking   dancing   fishing

Is handwriting your favourite hobby? Give yourself a tick.

Joining to small letters

How It Works

Are you ready for your first join? This one is all about joining to small letters from the bottom.

Start at the red dot. Follow the arrows and join the **a** to the **r**.

Now Try These

1. Practise this join by tracing and copying the letters below. Start at the red dot each time.

   ar   ar

   up   up

   ni   ni

2. Now try the same join, but from these tall letters.

   dr   dr

   lm   lm

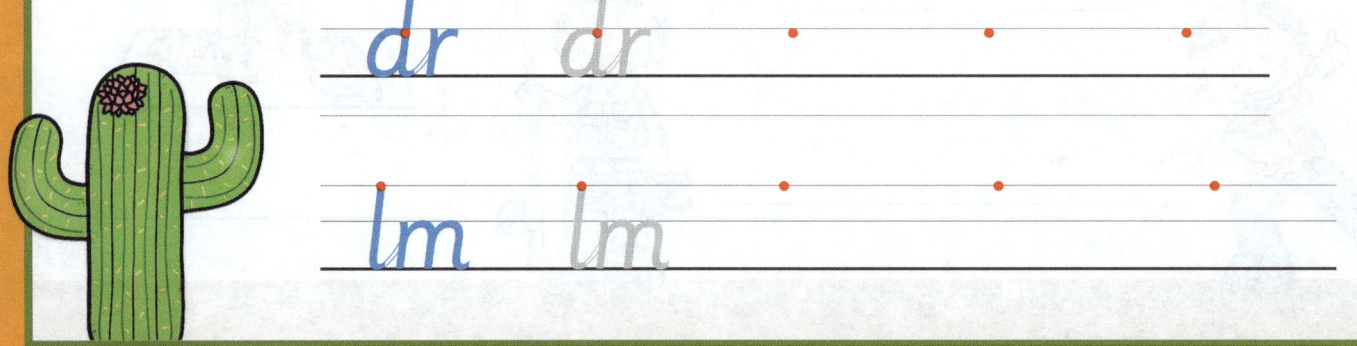

3. Can you write the first letter of each word? Make sure you join it properly to the next letter. Use the pictures to help you.

_ight   _ide   _irror

4. Trace and copy the words below to finish labelling the picture.

lip

hump

tummy

An Extra Challenge

Carl was doing some writing, but he accidentally used capital letters instead of joined up writing. Can you rewrite his words using joined up writing? Make sure you don't use any capital letters.

CUP   TINY   MUMMY

How did you find the first join?
Tick a box to show how you did.

Joining to e

How It Works

The letter **e** is really important because it's in lots and lots of words.

When you join to an **e** from the bottom of a letter, the **e** tilts slightly.

Start at the red dot and follow the arrows to try joining the **n** to the **e**.

Now Try These

1. Practise joining to **e** by tracing and copying the letters below.

   ne   ne

   ae   ae

   ke   ke

2. Some letters join to **e** from the top.
   Can you trace and then copy these joins?

   oe   oe

   fe   fe

3. You'll find the **ee** join in lots of words.
   Practise it by tracing the grey letters in the words below.

   sleep

   green   three

4. Can you trace and then copy these words?
   Remember that capital letters never join to other letters.

   deer in a line

   We are in a tree.

An Extra Challenge

Uh-oh! A naughty squirrel has stolen the letter **e** from each of the words below. Can you fill them in? Make sure you join them up to the letters on either side.

tim.   min   to   h n

rar   You'll need to add **ee** here. →   k n

Are you the bees knees at joining to e? Put a tick in a box.

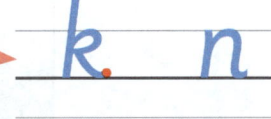

Joining small and tall letters

How It Works

This join links small letters to tall ones. It's sometimes called the second join.

See if you can trace it here. You'll need to start at the red dot and follow the arrows.

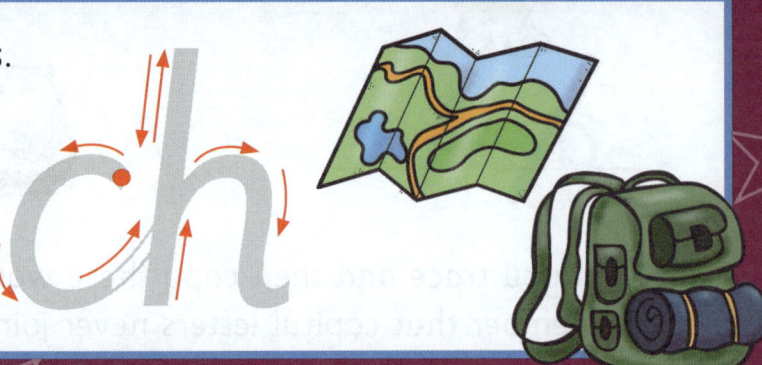

Now Try These

1. Practise the second join by tracing and copying the letters below.

   ch ch

   at at

   il il

2. You make the join between two tall letters in the same way. Have a go at tracing these words to practise.

   dull

   knelt

   wetter

   chilly

3. Can you trace and copy these words? Don't join up the capital letters.

We like a hike.

My feet feel wet.

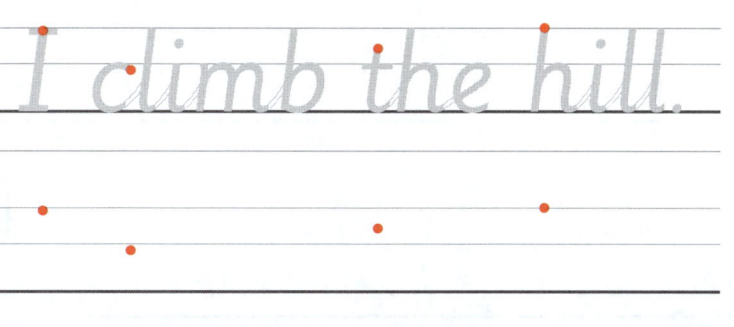

I climb the hill.

An Extra Challenge

Can you unscramble each group of letters to make a word? Write the words on the lines. Don't forget to join up the letters.

ntet

elfl

whce

Are you getting better at joining letters? Tick a box.

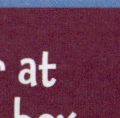   

Joining to round letters

How It Works

This join links to round letters like **o**, **a** and **s**. Some people call it the third join.

Follow the arrows to trace over the join between **n** and **o**.

You'll need to go back on yourself to do the **o**.

Now Try These

1. Practise joining to these round letters by tracing and copying them below.

   no no

   ea ea

   ng ng

2. When you're joining to **s**, the join is the same, but slightly longer. The **s** changes shape a little bit too. Give these letters a try.

   es es

   is is

3. Can you trace and copy these words?

He likes to dig.

This tree is tall.

They licked the ice creams.

An Extra Challenge

Arya has found a message in a bottle, but there are no spaces in between the words! Can you help her read the message by rewriting it with the spaces in the right places? The red dots show where each word starts.

hellothisismyllama

Were these pages a breeze?
Tick one of the boxes.

Joining from the top

How It Works

This join goes from the top of one letter to the top of the next. It's sometimes called the fourth join.

Have a go at tracing it here. Start at the red dot, then follow the arrows.

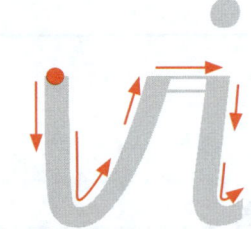

Now Try These

1. Practise joining from the top by tracing then copying these letters.

2. To join from **f** you need to lift your pencil off the page. Have a go at tracing and copying these letters.

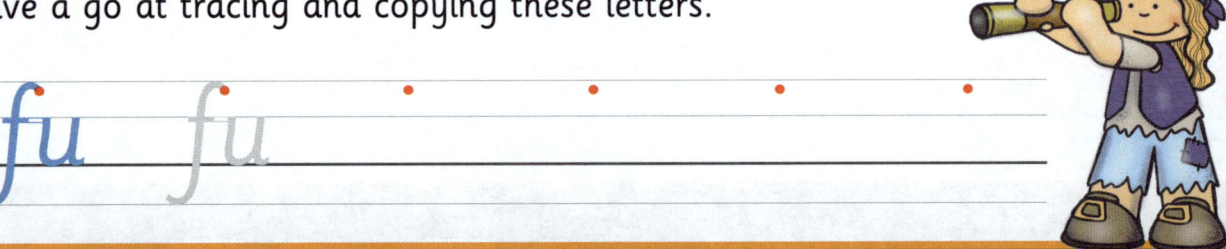

3. Can you trace and copy these words?

Your cannon fired.

Diving is fun.

The fins worry me.

An Extra Challenge

Patka's friend, Captain Onions, has left her a note to help her find his treasure, but some of the words have been washed away. Can you help Patka by writing the words from the blue box in the right places?

Onions
wreck
Four

Find the _____ of my ship, the _____.

How did it go? Is your handwriting ship-shape?

Distract the dragon

Jenna got lost inside an old, spooky castle, and now there's a scary dragon guarding the door! Solve the puzzles to work out a secret message — it will tell Jenna what she needs to do to escape the castle.

1. The first two words of the message are backwards. Can you rewrite the words the right way round?

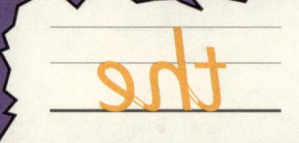

Don't forget to use joined up writing!

2. The next puzzle is in the library. Unscramble the letters on the books to find the next word in the message, then write it on the lines.

3. Jenna has found the next part of the message, but some letters are missing. Can you complete the two words below using the letters in the box?

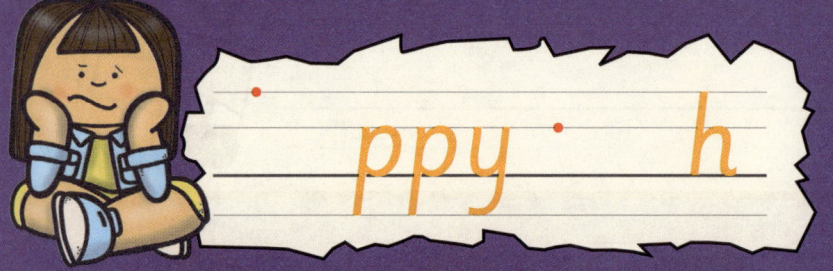

4. The next puzzle is tucked inside a suit of armour, but it doesn't make any sense! Could it be a code? Circle every third letter to spell out a word, then write it on the lines.

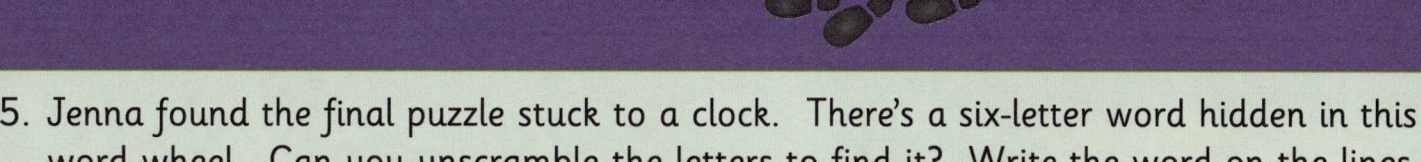

5. Jenna found the final puzzle stuck to a clock. There's a six-letter word hidden in this word wheel. Can you unscramble the letters to find it? Write the word on the lines.

6. Read all your answers to the puzzles in order. What should Jenna use to escape?

More joining from the top

How It Works

This join links the top of small letters to the middle of tall letters. It's known as the fifth join.

Can you trace the join between **o** and **b**? You need to go all the way to the bottom of the **b** before you go back up to do the round bit.

Now Try These

1. Practise this join by tracing and copying the letters below.

   ob ob

   rk rk

   ot ot

   wh wh

2. The join from the letter **f** is a bit different. Have a go at tracing these words.

   flip   fifth

   flaky   fluffy

3. Can you trace and copy the words below?

Add lots of white flour.

She turns off the hob.

I whip the cold cream.

An Extra Challenge

James saw something unexpected when he was cooking. He was so surprised that he got his words back to front. Rewrite each word with the letters in the right order to find out what James saw. Don't forget to join up the letters.

A elahw eta a elohw trat.

Were these pages a piece of cake? Give a box a tick.

More joining round letters

How It Works

Woo hoo! Just one more join to go. Some people call this one the sixth join.

For this join, you have to go back over a bit of the letter you've already drawn.

Try this out by tracing the join between **o** and **a**. Follow the arrows to help you.

Now Try These

1. Practise the sixth join by tracing and copying the letters below.

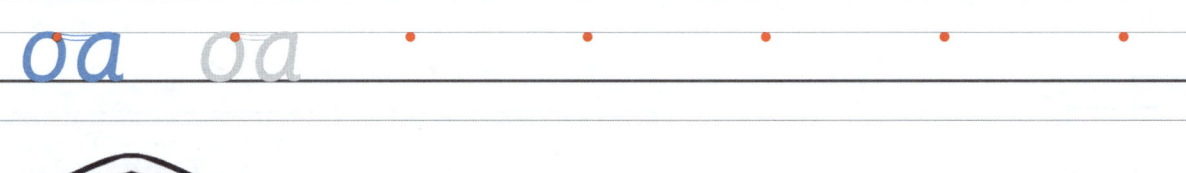

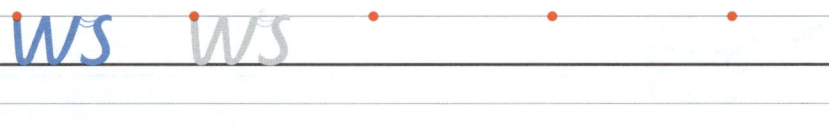

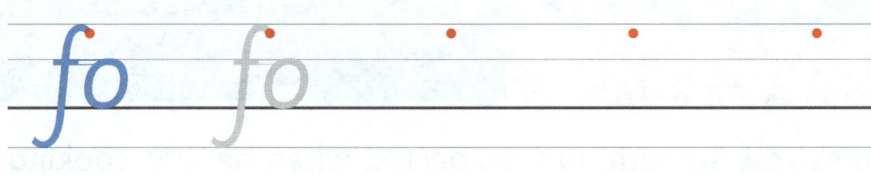

2. Now try joining to letters with tails. You make the join in the same way.

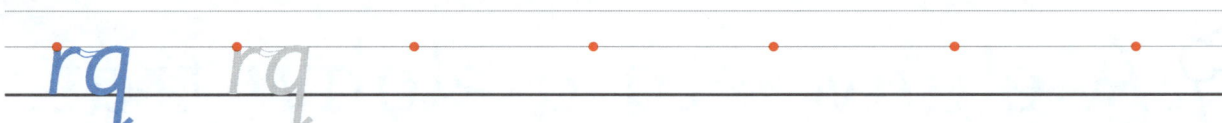

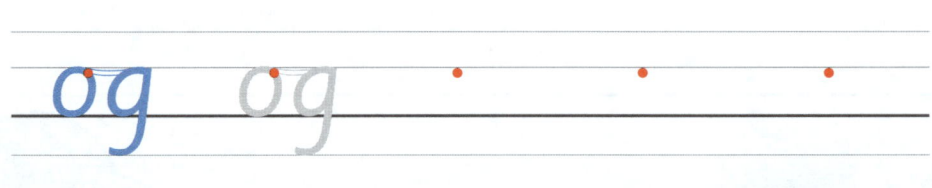

3. Trace the grey words below to practise making the sixth join.

dog

round

woof

wag

4. Can you trace and copy the words below? Start each word at the red dot.

The herd of cows moo.

A farmer walks in a wood.

An Extra Challenge

Can you rewrite these words using joined up writing? Make sure you don't use any capital letters.

CROP   OATS   FLOCK

How did it go? Did you plough through these pages?

Break letters

How It Works

Some letters don't join to the letter that comes after them. They're called break letters. The break letters are:

b g j p q s x y z

Now Try These

1. These words all start with break letters. Trace each word, then copy it out. Be careful — the letters are a bit smaller now.

   pile

   quick

   build

2. Now try tracing and copying these words that have break letters in the middle. Careful — there might be more than one break letter in a word.

   tape

   tyres

   sign

20

3. You don't join to or from the letters **x** and **z**.
   Practise these letters by tracing and copying the words below.

   fixes

   bulldozer

4. Now trace and copy these words.

   a dozen purple diggers

   My sister enjoys her job.

An Extra Challenge

Archie was reading the plans for a building when it started to rain. Some of the words got smudged and he can't read them. Can you help him by filling in the missing letters? Watch out for break letters!

icks

l   s ← There are two letters missing from these words.

a   e

Did you have a break letter breakthrough? Tick a box.

Capital letters

How It Works

Great job! It looks like you're really getting the hang of joined up writing. Now it's time to try some capital letters.

Capital letters never join to other letters.

Wanda   Leeds   Monday

Now Try These

1. Cedric is having a Halloween party and these are the friends that he wants to invite. Trace the names, then copy them out.

   Adam

   Zola

   Beth

2. Cedric needs to tell his friends when the party is. Can you trace and copy the words below?

   Friday

   October

3. Cedric needs to write his friends' addresses on the invitations. Trace and copy the place names below.

Adam

York

Zola

Perth

Beth

Rome

An Extra Challenge

Here is an advert for a tour of a haunted house. Some capital letters are missing. Circle the words that should have a capital letter. Can you rewrite them on the lines without any mistakes?

Spookton Manor

Come and visit the most haunted house in england — if you're brave enough!

On saturday the 1st of november, there will be a special tour of the house. Join us if you dare!

Are capital letters a treat? Or are they just tricky? Tick a box.

A trip to the supermarket

How It Works

Now that you're a pro at joined up writing, it's time to put your new skills into practice.

Remember — break letters and capital letters don't join to the letter that comes after them.

Now Try These

1. Malik's dad has asked him to write out their shopping list before they go to the supermarket. Can you trace and then copy the list?

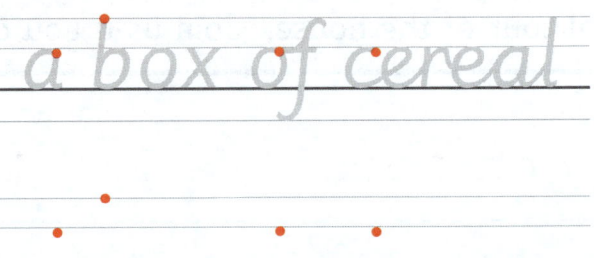

2. Malik is describing his favourite meal. Trace over these words, filling in any gaps as you go. Use the pictures to help you.

I like roast chicken with

carrots, potatoes and peas.

I have a glass of milk.

For pudding, I usually

eat a strawberry yoghurt.

An Extra Challenge

Malik wants to sneak a few more things onto the shopping list, but he can't remember how to spell them. Can you help him unscramble the letters, then write the words on the lines? Use the pictures to help you.

o h l c e
c o a t

e t s
w e s

z p
z i a

_____   _____   _____

Were you super at this page?
Tick a box to show how you did.

Build your own robot

How It Works

You're well on your way to becoming a real handwriting expert!

Put your joined up writing to the test with these sentences about robots.

Now Try These

1. Here are some instructions on how to build a robot. Can you trace them and then copy them out?

First, put the head carefully

onto the body. Attach the legs.

Your robot is ready to go.

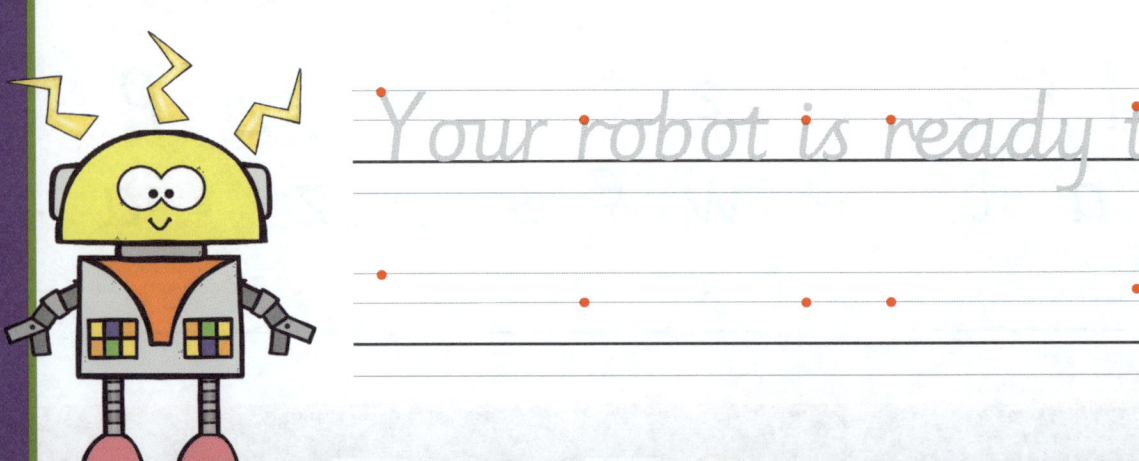

2. Copy out each sentence, filling in the gap with the missing number. Use the pictures to help you. You should write out the numbers in words.

Max has ? arms.

Aqua has ? feet.

Pod has ? wheels.

An Extra Challenge

Uh-oh! Reggie the Writing Robot is broken and he keeps using mirror writing. Can you rewrite these words the right way round?

buzz   screw    metal

Are you wheel-y good at joined up writing? Tick a box.

Space stories

How It Works

Great work! You made it to the last bit of handwriting practice!

It's time to show off your amazing handwriting skills, so each line only has one red dot which tells you where to start the first word.

Now Try These

1. Here are some facts about space. Trace each sentence, then copy it out.

We live on planet Earth.

The Sun is a type of star.

Space is cold and very big.

2. Here is the beginning of a story about an astronaut. Can you copy it out on the lines below?

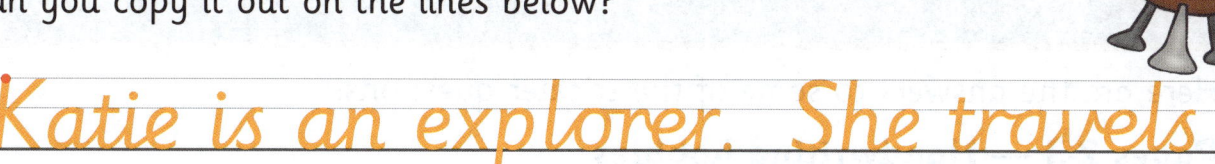

Katie is an explorer. She travels through space in a small rocket and meets friendly aliens.

An Extra Challenge

Zarb is one of Katie's alien friends. He wants to use joined up writing, but he doesn't know how. Can you show him how to write these words?

moon   comet   Zarb

Are you a star at handwriting?
Tick a box to show how you did.

Answers

Here are the answers to some of the trickier questions:

Pages 2-3 — Handwriting hobbies
An Extra Challenge

 dancing  fishing  baking

Pages 8-9 — Joining small and tall letters
An Extra Challenge

 tent  fell  chew

Pages 12-13 — Joining from the top
An Extra Challenge

Find the wreck of my ship, the Four Onions.

Pages 14-15 — Distract the dragon

1. keep the
2. dragon
3. happy with
4. tasty
5. apples
6. c) — the apples

Pages 20-21 — Break letters
An Extra Challenge

 logs  bricks  axe

Pages 22-23 — Capital letters
An Extra Challenge

England Saturday November

Pages 24-25 — A trip to the supermarket
An Extra Challenge

 chocolate  sweets  pizza